Hopscotch

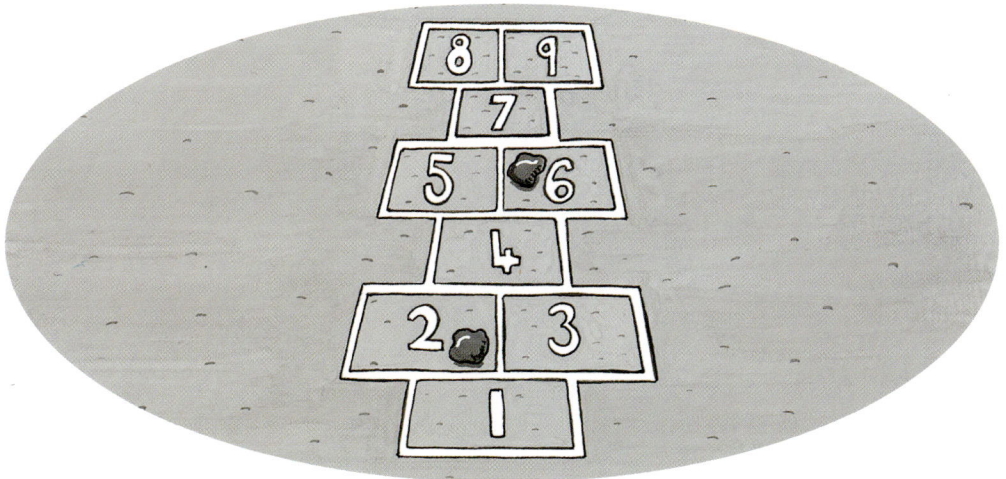

Written by Sue Mayfield

Illustrated by Tracey English

Rigby

We like to hop.

Hop
   down
      the street.

Hop to the shop.

Hop back home
with a bottle of pop.

Keep on hopping!
Must not stop!

Hop to the top.
Hop till you drop.

Time for a drink!
Open the pop!

Ooops! What a mess!
Get me a mop!